Poems of Love and Life for
VIRGO
(24 AUGUST to 22 SEPTEMBER)

JULIA & DEREK PARKER

EBURY
PRESS

Every effort has been made to acknowledge and contact the copyright holders for permission to reproduce material contained in this book. Any copyright holders who have been inadvertently omitted from acknowledgements and credits should contact the publisher and omissions will be rectified in subsequent editions.

An Ebury Press book
Published by Random House Australia Pty Ltd
Level 3, 100 Pacific Highway, North Sydney NSW 2060
www.randomhouse.com.au

First published by Ebury Press in 2013

Copyright © Julia & Derek Parker 2013

The moral right of the authors has been asserted.

All rights reserved. No part of this book may be reproduced or transmitted by any person or entity, including internet search engines or retailers, in any form or by any means, electronic or mechanical, including photocopying (except under the statutory exceptions provisions of the Australian *Copyright Act 1968*), recording, scanning or by any information storage and retrieval system without the prior written permission of Random House Australia.

Addresses for companies within the Random House Group can be found at
www.randomhouse.com.au/offices

National Library of Australia
Cataloguing-in-Publication entry (pbk.)

Parker, Julia, 1932–
Poems of love and life for Virgo/Julia and Derek Parker.

ISBN 978 1 74275 785 8 (pbk.)

Virgo (Astrology) – Poetry
Love poetry

Other Authors/Contributors:
Parker, Derek, 1932–

133.5267

Cover illustration by Rhian Nest James
Cover design by Cathie Glassby
Internal design and typesetting by Midland Typesetters, Australia
Printed in Australia by Griffin Press, an accredited ISO AS/NZS 14001:2004 Environmental Management System printer

Random House Australia uses papers that are natural, renewable and recyclable products and made from wood grown in sustainable forests. The logging and manufacturing processes are expected to conform to the environmental regulations of the country of origin.

TO ALL LOVERS OF POETRY AND ASTROLOGY

Introduction

In this book we have collected together poems which we believe will appeal to readers born between 24 August and 22 September, and therefore think of themselves as 'Virgos' and read the paragraphs printed under *Virgo* in newspaper and magazine astrology columns.

These are based on the idea of 'Sun-sign' or 'Star-sign' astrology – a very recent one, invented in the 1930s by an astrological journalist who wanted to simplify the extremely complex system used by professional astrologers over at least two thousand years of history. Though this may seem a very simple idea, it is all the same true that you and other people born when the Sun is 'in' Virgo – that is, stands between the Earth and a particular background of sky – do share certain characteristics.

Virgos are, for instance, generally speaking discriminating and fastidious, and Pope's *On A Certain Lady At Court* (p.1) is a perfect description of a Virgoan woman. Modesty is a strong characteristic much to the fore in the early stages of relationships –

Matthew Prior (p.21 – though is she entirely honest in her protestations?), Moore's *Did Not* (p.20), and Story's *Snowdrop* (p.11) echo this theme. Virgoans love their gardens, plants, country landscapes – see Austin Dobson (p.81) and A. Tennyson (p.65). *On An Island* (p.46) underlines their need to be kept busy, and their capacity for hard work is shown in Mary Gilmore's rather sad *Marri'd* (p.44) and more amusingly in Louisa May Alcott's *A Song From The Suds* (p.47).

Often over-critical and with a tendency to nag, Virgoans could take a lesson from Hardy's *She Charged Me* (p.30), while *Why Don't The Men Propose* (p.49) suggests a certain air of Virgoan desperation. They enjoy hobbies and gossip (p.112), and their love of small animals is delightfully expressed in Wordsworth's *See The Kitten On The Wall* (p.113) and Yeats's *The Cat And The Moon* (p.116). Holmes's *My Aunt* (p.100), is a sad but perhaps accurate sketch of an Virgoan spinster of an earlier age.

These poems are chosen because they reflect your attitude to life, your character and your interests, and also because they are associated with seasons, countries, towns which are (in astrological terms) 'ruled' by the sign. The chances are that you will identify with many of their themes. Some we have chosen simply because we believe you will enjoy them, and that they will awaken or re-awaken your love of poetry.

J. P. & D. P.
Sydney, 2012

On A Certain Lady At Court

I know a thing that's most uncommon;
(Envy, be silent and attend!)
I know a reasonable woman,
Handsome and witty, yet a friend.

Not warped by passion, awed by rumour;
Not grave through pride, nor gay through folly;
An equal mixture of good-humour
And sensible soft melancholy.

'Has she no faults, then (Envy says), Sir?'
Yes, she has one, I must aver:
When all the world conspires to praise her,
The woman's deaf, and does not hear.

– Alexander Pope

Good Counsel To A Young Maid

Gaze not on thy beauty's pride,
Tender maid, in the false tide
That from lovers' eyes doth slide.

Let thy faithful crystal show
How thy colours come and go:
Beauty takes a foil from woe.

Love, that in those smooth streams lies
Under pity's fair disguise,
Will thy melting heart surprise.

Nets of passion's finest thread,
Snaring poems, will be spread,
All to catch thy maidenhead.

Then beware! for those that cure
Love's disease, themselves endure
For reward a calenture[1].

---

1 calenture – fever

Rather let the lover pine,
Than his pale cheek should assign
A perpetual blush to thine.

– *Thomas Carew*

Love's Infiniteness

If yet I have not all thy love,
Dear, I shall never have it all,
I cannot breathe one other sigh, to move,
Nor can entreat one other tear to fall,
And all my treasure, which should purchase thee,
Sighs, tears, and oaths, and letters I have spent.
Yet no more can be due to me,
Than at the bargain made was meant;
If then thy gift of love were partial,
That some to me, some should to others fall,
Dear, I shall never have thee all.

Or if then thou gavest me all,
All was but all, which thou hadst then;
But if in thy heart, since, there be or shall
New love created be, by other men,
Which have their stocks entire, and can in tears,
In sighs, in oaths, and letters outbid me,
This new love may beget new fears,
For, this love was not vowed by thee.
And yet it was, thy gift being general;

The ground, thy heart, is mine, whatever shall
Grow there, dear, I should have it all.

Yet I would not have all yet;
He that hath all can have no more,
And since my love doth every day admit
New growth, thou shouldst have new rewards in store;
Thou canst not every day give me thy heart,
If thou canst give it, then thou never gavest it:
Love's riddles are, that though thy heart depart,
It stays at home, and thou with losing savest it:
But we will have a way more liberal,
Than changing hearts, to join them, so we shall
Be one, and one another's all.

— *John Donne*

Women

When lovely woman stoops to folly,
    And finds too late that men betray,
What charm can soothe her melancholy?
    What art can wash her tears away?

The only art her guilt to cover,
    To hide her shame from every eye,
To give repentance to her lover,
    And wring his bosom is – to die.

– Oliver Goldsmith

When We Shall Be Dust

When we shall be dust in the churchyard –
    In twenty years – in fifty years –
Who will remember you kissed me once,
    Who will be grieved for our tears?

The locust tree will have grown taller,
    The old walks will be covered with grass,
And past our quiet graves go straying
    A youth with his arm round his lass.

And the bee that shall suck your grave flowers –
    Anemone, stock, columbine,
May pause in his swift homing journey
    To taste of the honey from mine.

– Muna Lee

Sonnet

I said I splendidly loved you; it's not true.
    Such long swift tides stir not a land-locked sea.
On gods or fools the high risk falls – on you –
    The clean clear bitter-sweet that's not for me.
Love soars from earth to ecstasies unwist[1].
    Love is flung Lucifer-like from Heaven to Hell.
But – there are wanderers in the middle mist,
    Who cry for shadows, clutch, and cannot tell
Whether they love at all, or, loving, whom:
    An old song's lady, a fool in fancy dress,
Or phantoms, or their own face on the gloom;
    For love of Love, or from heart's loneliness.
Pleasure's not theirs, nor pain. They doubt, and sigh,
    And do not love at all. Of these am I.

– Rupert Brooke

---

1 unwist – unknown

Love Is A Terrible Thing

I went out to the farthest meadow,
I lay down in the deepest shadow;

And I said unto the earth, 'Hold me,'
And unto the night, 'O enfold me,'

And unto the wind petulantly
I cried, 'You know not for you are free!'

And I begged the little leaves to lean
Low and together for a safe screen;

Then to the stars I told my tale:
'That is my home-light, there in the vale,

'And O, I know that I shall return,
But let me lie first mid the unfeeling fern.

'For there is a flame that has blown too near,
And there is a name that has grown too dear,
And there is a fear …'

And to the still hills and cool earth and far sky I made
    moan,
'The heart in my bosom is not my own!

'O would I were free as the wind on wing;
Love is a terrible thing!'

– *Grace Fallow Norton*

Snowdrop

When, full of warm and eager love,
    I clasp you in my fond embrace,
You gently push me back and say,
    'Take care, my dear, you'll spoil my lace.'

You kiss me just as you would kiss
    Some woman friend you chanced to see;
You call me 'dearest.' – All love's forms
    Are yours, not its reality.

Oh, Annie! cry, and storm, and rave!
    Do anything with passion in it!
Hate me an hour, and then turn round
    And love me truly, just one minute.

– *William Wetmore Story*

Song

Still to be neat, still to be dressed,
As you were going to a feast;
Still to be powdered, still perfumed:
Lady, it is to be presumed,
Though art's hid causes are not found,
All is not sweet, all is not sound.

Give me a look, give me a face,
That makes simplicity a grace;
Robes loosely flowing, hair as free:
Such sweet neglect more taketh me
Than all the adulteries of art;
They strike mine eyes, but not my heart.

– *Ben Jonson*

I Fear Thy Kisses

I fear thy kisses, gentle maiden;
Thou needest not fear mine;
My spirit is too deeply laden
Ever to burthen thine.

I fear thy mien, thy tones, thy motion;
Thou needest not fear mine;
Innocent is the heart's devotion
With which I worship thine.

– Percy Bysshe Shelley

Song

O blush not so! O blush not so!
    Or I shall think you knowing;
And if you smile, the blushing while,
    Then maidenheads are going.

There's a blush for won't, and a blush for shan't,
    And a blush for having done it;
There's a blush for thought, and a blush for nought,
    And a blush for just begun it.

O sigh not so! O sigh not so!
    For it sounds of Eve's sweet pippin;
By those loosened hips, you have tasted the pips,
    And fought in an amorous nipping.

Will you play once more, at nice cut-core,
    For it only will last our youth out;
And we have the prime of the kissing time,
    We have not one sweet tooth out.

There's a sigh for yes, and a sigh for no,
    And a sigh for I can't bear it!
O what can be done? Shall we stay or run?
    O cut the sweet apple and share it!

– John Keats

Her Pity

This is the room to which she came that day –
Came when the dusk was falling cold and grey –
Came with soft step, in delicate array,

And sat beside me in the firelight there;
And, like a rose of perfume rich and rare,
Thrilled with her sweetness the environing air.

We heard the grind of traffic in the street,
The clamorous calls, the beat of passing feet,
The wail of bells that in the twilight meet.

Then I knelt down, and dared to touch her hand –
Those slender fingers, and the shining band
Of happy gold wherewith her wrist was spanned.

Her radiant beauty made my heart rejoice;
And then she spoke, and her low, pitying voice
Was like the soft, pathetic, tender noise

Of winds that come before a summer rain:
Once leaped the blood in every clamorous vein;
Once leaped my heart, then, dumb, stood still again.

— *Philip Bourke Marston*

Love's Spite

You take a town you cannot keep;
And, forced in turn to fly,
O'er ruins you have made shall leap
Your deadliest enemy!
Her love is yours – and be it so –
But can you keep it? No, no, no!

Upon her brow we gazed with awe,
And loved, and wished to love, in vain,
But when the snow begins to thaw
We shun with scorn the miry plain.
Women with grace may yield: but she
Appeared some Virgin Deity.

Bright was her soul as Dian's crest
Whitening on Vesta's fane[1] its sheen:
Cold looked she as the waveless breast

---

[1] Vesta's fane – the goddess' temple

Of some stone Diana at thirteen.
Men loved: but hope they deemed to be
A sweet impossibility!

– Aubrey de Vere

Did Not

'Twas a new feeling – something more
Than we had dared to own before,
Which then we hid not, which then we hid not.
We saw it in each other's eye,
And wished, in every murmured sigh,
To speak, but did not; to speak, but did not.

She felt my lips' impassioned touch –
'Twas the first time I dared so much,
And yet she chid not, and yet she chid not;
But whispered o'er my burning brow,
O! do you doubt I love you now?
Sweet soul! I did not; sweet soul! I did not.

Warmly I felt her bosom thrill,
I pressed it closer, closer still,
Though gently bid not, though gently bid not;
Till – oh! the world hath seldom heard
Of lovers, who so nearly erred,
And yet who did not, and yet who did not.

– *Thomas Moore*

A Song

For God's sake – nay, dear Sir,
Lord, what do you mean?
I protest and I vow, Sir,
Your ways are obscene.

Pray give o'er; O, fie,
Pish, leave off your fooling,
Forbear, or I'll cry –
I hate this rude doing.

Let me die if I stay –
Does the Devil possess you?
Your hand take away,
Then perhaps I may bless you.

– Matthew Prior

No Loathsomeness In Love

What I fancy I approve,
No dislike there is in love:
Be my mistress short or tall,
And distorted therewithal:
Be she likewise one of those,
That an acre hath of nose:
Be her forehead and her eyes
Full of incongruities:
Be her cheeks so shallow too,
As to show her tongue wag through;
Be her lips ill hung or set,
And her grinders black as jet:
Hath she thin hair, hath she none,
She's to me a paragon.

– Robert Herrick

Nymph

Nymph of the downward smile, and sidelong glance,
In what diviner moments of the day
Art thou most lovely? When gone far astray
Into the labyrinths of sweet utterance?
Or when serenely wandering in a trance
Of sober thought? Or when starting away,
With careless robe, to meet the morning ray,
Thou sparest the flowers in thy mazy dance?
Haply 'tis when thy ruby lips part sweetly,
And so remain, because thou listenest:
But thou to please wert nurtured so completely
That I can never tell what mood is best.
I shall as soon pronounce which grace more neatly
Trips it before Apollo than the rest.

– John Keats

If They Asked Me, I Could Write A Book

A-B-C-D-E-F-G
I never learned to spell –
at least not well.
1-2-3-4-5-6-7
I never learned to count
a great amount.
But my busy mind is burning
to use what learning I've got –
I won't waste any time –
I'll strike while the iron is hot.

If they asked me, I could write a book
about the way you walk and whisper and look.
I could write a preface on how we met
so the world would never forget.
And the simple secret of the plot
is just to tell them that I love you a lot.
Then the world discovers as my book ends
how to make two lovers of friends.

– Lorenz Hart

If Love The Virgin's Heart Invade

If love the virgin's heart invade,
How, like a moth, the simple maid
Still plays about the flame!
If soon she be not made a wife,
Her honour's singed, and then for life,
She's – what I dare not name.

– *John Gay*

Louisa

(After accompanying her on a mountain excursion.)

I met Louisa in the shade,
And, having seen that lovely maid,
Why should I fear to say
That, nymph-like, she is fleet and strong,
And down the rocks can leap along
Like rivulets in May?

She loves her fire, her cottage-home;
Yet o'er the moorland will she roam
In weather rough and bleak;
And, when against the wind she strains,
Oh! might I kiss the mountain rains
That sparkle on her cheek.

Take all that's mine beneath the moon,
If I with her but half a noon
May sit beneath the walls
Of some old cave, or mossy nook,
When up she winds along the brook
To hunt the waterfalls.

– *William Wordsworth*

The Young Man In April

In the queer light, in twilight,
In April of the year,
I meet a thousand women,
But I never meet my Dear.
Yet each of them has something,
A turn of neck or knee,
A line of breast or shoulder,
That brings my Dear to me.

One has a way of swaying,
I'd swear to anywhere;
One has a laugh, and one a hat,
And one a trick of hair;
 – Oh, glints and hints and gestures,
When shall I find complete
The Dear that's walking somewhere,
The Dear I've yet to meet?

– *Rupert Brooke*

O That 'Twere Possible

O that 'twere possible
After long grief and pain
To find the arms of my true love
Round me once again! ...

A shadow flits before me,
Not thou, but like to thee:
Ah, Christ! that it were possible
For one short hour to see
The souls we loved, that they might tell us
What and where they be!

– *Alfred, Lord Tennyson*

She Charged Me

She charged me with having said this and that
To another woman long years before,
In the very parlour where we sat, –

Sat on a night when the endless pour
Of rain on the roof and the road below
Bent the spring of the spirit more and more ...

– So charged she me; and the Cupids bow
Of her mouth was hard, and her eyes, and her face,
And her white forefinger lifted slow.

Had she done it gently, or shown a trace
That not too curiously would she view
A folly passed ere her reign had place,

A kiss might have ended it. But I knew
From the fall of each word, and the pause between,
That the curtain would drop upon us two
Ere long, in our play of slave and queen.

– *Thomas Hardy*

Being Your Slave, What Should I Do?

Being your slave, what should I do but tend
Upon the hours and times of your desire?
I have no precious time at all to spend,
Nor services to do, till you require.
Nor dare I chide the world-without-end hour
Whilst I, my sovereign, watch the clock for you,
Nor think the bitterness of absence sour
When you have bid your servant once adieu;
Nor dare I question with my jealous thought
Where you may be, or your affairs suppose,
But, like a sad slave, stay and think of nought
Save, where you are how happy you make those.
    So true a fool is love that in your will,
      Though you do anything, he thinks no ill.

– William Shakespeare

Phillida And Corydon

♍

Fair in a morn (O fairest morn!),
Was never morn so fair,
There shone a sun, though not the sun
That shineth in the air.
For the earth, and from the earth,
(Was never such a creature!)
Did come this face (was never face
That carried such a feature).
Upon a hill (O blessèd hill!
Was never hill so blessèd),
There stood a man (was never man
For woman so distressèd):
This man beheld a heavenly view,
Which did such virtue give
As clears the blind, and helps the lame,
And makes the dead man live.
This man had hap (O happy man!
More happy none than he);
For he had hap to see the hap
That none had hap to see.
This silly swain (and silly swains

Are men of meanest grace):
Had yet the grace (O gracious gift!)
To hap on such a face.

He pity cried, and pity came
And pitied so his pain,
As dying would not let him die
But gave him life again.
For joy whereof he made such mirth
As all the woods did ring;
And Pan with all his swains came forth
To hear the shepherd sing;
But such a song sung never was,
Nor shall be sung again,
Of Phyllida the shepherds' queen,
And Corydon the swain.
Fair Phyllis is the shepherds' queen,
(Was never such a queen as she)
And Corydon her only swain
(Was never such a swain as he):
Fair Phyllis hath the fairest face
That ever eye did yet behold,
And Corydon the constant'st faith
That ever yet kept flock in fold;

Since then that Phyllis only is
The only shepherd's only queen;
And Corydon the only swain
That only hath her shepherd been, –
Though Phyllis keep her bower of state,

Shall Corydon consume away?
No, shepherd, no, work out the week,
And Sunday shall be holiday.

– *Nicholas Breton*

Hear, Ye Ladies

Hear, ye ladies that despise
    What the mighty Love has done;
Fear examples and be wise:
    Fair Callisto was a nun;
Leda, sailing on the stream
    To deceive the hopes of man,
Love accounting but a dream,
    Doted on a silver swan;
        Danaëe, in a brazen tower,
        Where no love was, loved a shower.

Hear, ye ladies that are coy,
    What the mighty Love can do;
Fear the fierceness of the boy:
    The chaste Moon he makes to woo;
Vesta, kindling holy fires,
    Circled round about with spies,

Never dreaming loose desires,
    Doting at the altar dies;
        Ilion[1], in a short hour, higher
        He can build, and once more fire.

– *John Fletcher*

---

1 Ilion – an ancient name for Troy

Love's Coming

Quietly as rosebuds
Talk to thin air,
Love came so lightly
I knew not he was there.

Quietly as lovers
Creep at the middle noon,
Softly as players tremble
In the tears of a tune;

Quietly as lilies
Their faint vows declare,
Came the shy pilgrim:
I knew not he was there.

Quietly as tears fall
On a warm sin,
Softly as griefs call
In a violin;

Without hail or tempest,
Blue sword or flame,
Love came so lightly
I knew not that he came.

– *John Shaw Neilson*

A Woman's Question

Before I trust my fate to thee,
Or place my hand in thine,
Before I let thy future give
Colour and form to mine,
Before I peril all for thee, question thy soul to-night
    for me.

I break all slighter bonds, nor feel
A shadow of regret:
Is there one link within the past
That holds thy spirit yet?
Or is thy faith as clear and free as that which I can
    pledge to thee?

Does there within thy dimmest dreams
A possible future shine,
Wherein thy life could henceforth breathe,
Untouched, unshared by mine?
If so, at any pain or cost, O, tell me before all is lost.

Look deeper still. If thou canst feel,
Within thy inmost soul,
That thou hast kept a portion back,
While I have staked the whole,
Let no false pity spare the blow, but in true mercy tell
    me so.

Is there within thy heart a need
That mine cannot fulfil?
One chord that any other hand
Could better wake or still?
Speak now – lest at some future day my whole life
    wither and decay.

Lives there within thy nature hid
The demon-spirit change,
Shedding a passing glory still
On all things new and strange?
It may not be thy fault alone, – but shield my heart
    against thy own.

Couldst thou withdraw thy hand one day
And answer to my claim,
That Fate, and that to-day's mistake –
Not thou – had been to blame?
Some soothe their conscience thus; but thou wilt
    surely warn and save me now.

Nay, answer not, – I dare not hear,
The words would come too late;
Yet I would spare thee all remorse,
So, comfort thee, my Fate, –
Whatever on my heart may fall – remember, I would
    risk it all!

– Adelaide Anne Procter

Love's Philosophy

The fountains mingle with the river,
And the rivers with the ocean;
The winds of heaven mix forever,
With a sweet emotion;
Nothing in the world is single;
All things by a law divine
In one another's being mingle;
Why not I with thine?

See! the mountains kiss high heaven,
And the waves clasp one another;
No sister flower would be forgiven,
If it disdained its brother;
And the sunlight clasps the earth,
And the moonbeams kiss the sea;
What are all these kissings worth,
If thou kiss not me?

– *Percy Bysshe Shelley*

Marri'd

It's singin' in an' out,
An' feelin' full of grace;
Here 'n' there, up an' down,
An' round about th' place.

It's rollin' up your sleeves,
An' whit'nin' up the hearth,
An' scrubbin' out th' floors,
An' sweepin' down th' path;

It's bakin' tarts an' pies,
An' shinin' up th' knives;
An' feelin' 's if some days
Was worth a thousand lives.

It's watchin' out th' door,
An' watchin' by th' gate;
An' watchin' down th' road,
An' wonderin' why he's late;

An' feelin' anxious-like,
For fear there's something wrong;
An' wonderin' why he's kep',
An' why he takes so long.

It's comin' back inside
An' sittin' down a spell,
To sort of make believe
You're thinkin' things is well.

It's gettin' up again
An' wand'rin' in an' out;
An' feelin' wistful-like,
Not knowin' what about;

An' flushin' all at once,
An' smilin' just so sweet,
An' feelin' *real* proud
The place is fresh an' neat.

An' feelin' awful glad
Like them that watch'd Silo'm;
An' everything because
A man is comin' Home!

– Mary Gilmore

On An Island

You've plucked a curlew, drawn a hen,
Washed the shirts of seven men,
You've stuffed my pillow, stretched my sheet,
And filled the pan to wash your feet,
You've cooped the pullets, wound the clock,
And rinsed the young men's drinking crock;
And now we'll dance to jigs and reels,
Nailed boots chasing girl's naked heels,
Until your father'll start to snore,
And Jude, now you're married, will stretch on the floor.

– J. M. Synge

A Song From The Suds

Queen of my tub, I merrily sing,
While the white foam raises high,
And sturdily wash, and rinse, and wring,
And fasten the clothes to dry;
Then out in the free fresh air they swing,
Under the sunny sky.

I wish we could wash from our hearts and our souls
The stains of the week away,
And let water and air by their magic make
Ourselves as pure as they;
Then on the earth there would be indeed
A glorious washing day!

Along the path of a useful life
Will heart's-ease ever bloom;
The busy mind has no time to think
Of sorrow, or care, or gloom;
And anxious thoughts may be swept away
As we busily wield a broom.

I am glad a task to me is given
To labour at day by day;
For it brings me health, and strength, and hope,
And I cheerfully learn to say –
'Head, you may think; heart, you may feel;
But hand, you shall work always!'

– Louisa May Alcott

Why Don't The Men Propose

Why don't the men propose, mamma?
    Why *don't* the men propose?
Each seems just coming to the point,
    And then away he goes!
It is no fault of yours, mamma,
    That everybody knows;
You *fête* the finest men in town,
    Yet, oh! they won't propose!

I'm sure I've done my best, mamma,
    To make a proper match;
For coronets and eldest sons
    I'm ever on the watch;
I've hopes when some *distingué* beau
    A glance upon me throws;
But though he'll dance, and smile, and flirt,
    Alas! he won't propose!

I've tried to win by languishing
    And dressing like a blue;
I've bought big books, and talked of them
    As *if* I'd read them through!
With hair cropped like a man, I've felt
    The heads of all the beaux;
But Spurzheim[1] could not touch their *hearts*,
    And, oh! they won't propose!

I threw aside the books, and thought
    That ignorance was bliss;
I felt convinced that men preferred
    A simple sort of Miss;
And so I lisped out naught beyond
    Plain 'Yeses' or plain 'noes,'
And wore a sweet unmeaning smile;
    Yet, oh! they won't propose!

Last night, at Lady Ramble's rout,
    I heard Sir Harry Gale
Exclaim, 'Now I *propose* again!'
    I started, turning pale;
I really thought my time was come,
    I blushed like any rose;
But, oh! I found 't was only at
    Ecarté[2] he'd *propose*!

---

1 Spurzheim – a popular phrenologist
2 *ecarté* – a card game

And what is to be done, mamma?
    Oh! what is to be done?
I really have no time to lose,
    For I am thirty-one:
At balls I am too often left
    Where spinsters sit in rows;
Why won't the men propose, mamma?
    Why *won't* the men propose?

– Thomas Haynes Bayly

O Fairest Of The Rural Maids

Oh fairest of the rural maids!
Thy birth was in the forest shades;
Green boughs, and glimpses of the sky,
Were all that met thy infant eye.

Thy sports, thy wanderings, when a child,
Were ever in the sylvan wild;
And all the beauty of the place
Is in thy heart and on thy face.

The twilight of the trees and rocks
Is in the light shade of thy locks;
Thy step is as the wind, that weaves
Its playful way among the leaves.

Thine eyes are springs, in whose serene
And silent waters heaven is seen;
Their lashes are the herbs that look
On their young figures in the brook.

The forest depths, by foot unpressed,
Are not more sinless than thy breast;
The holy peace, that fills the air
Of those calm solitudes, is there.

— *William Cullen Bryant*

The Maid Of Llanwellyn

I've no sheep on the mountains
Nor boat on the lake
Nor coin in my coffer
To keep me awake
Nor corn in my garner,
Nor fruit on my tree
Yet the maid of Llanwellyn
Smiles sweetly on me.

Rich Owen will tell you,
With eyes full of scorn
Threadbare is my coat,
And my hosen are torn
Scoff on, my rich Owen,
For faint is thy glee
When the maid of Llanwellyn
Smiles sweetly on me.

The farmer rides proudly
To market and fair
And the clerk at the ale house
Still claims the great chair;
But of all our proud fellows,
The proudest I'll be
While the maid of Llanwellyn
Smiles sweetly on me.

– Joanna Baillie

I Stood Tip-Toe

I stood tip-toe upon a little hill,
The air was cooling, and so very still,
That the sweet buds which with a modest pride
Pull droopingly, in slanting curve aside,
Their scantly leaved, and finely tapering stems,
Had not yet lost those starry diadems
Caught from the early sobbing of the morn.
The clouds were pure and white as flocks new shorn,
And fresh from the clear brook; sweetly they slept
On the blue fields of heaven, and then there crept
A little noiseless noise among the leaves,
Born of the very sigh that silence heaves:
For not the faintest motion could be seen
Of all the shades that slanted o'er the green.
There was wide wandering for the greediest eye,
To peer about upon variety;
Far round the horizon's crystal air to skim,
And trace the dwindled edgings of its brim;

To picture out the quaint, and curious bending
Of a fresh woodland alley, never ending;
Or by the bowery clefts, and leafy shelves,
Guess where the jaunty streams refresh themselves.

– John Keats

Gathering Leaves

Spades take up leaves
No better than spoons,
And bags full of leaves
Are light as balloons.

I make a great noise
Of rustling all day
Like rabbit and deer
Running away.

But the mountains I raise
Elude my embrace,
Flowing over my arms
And into my face.

I may load and unload
Again and again
Till I fill the whole shed,
And what have I then?

Next to nothing for weight,
And since they grew duller
From contact with earth,
Next to nothing for colour.

Next to nothing for use.
But a crop is a crop,
And who's to say where
The harvest shall stop?

– *Robert Frost*

To A Young Lady Who Had Been Reproached For Taking Long Walks In The Country

Dear child of nature, let them rail!
– There is a nest in a green dale,
A harbour and a hold;
Where thou, a wife and friend, shalt see
Thy own heart-stirring days, and be
A light to young and old.

There, healthy as a shepherd boy,
And treading among flowers of joy
Which at no season fade,
Thou, while thy babes around thee cling,
Shalt show us how divine a thing
A woman may be made.

Thy thoughts and feelings shall not die,
Nor leave thee, when grey hairs are nigh,
A melancholy slave;
But an old age serene and bright,
And lovely as a Lapland night,
Shall lead thee to thy grave.

– *William Wordsworth*

The Woodland Halló

In our cottage, that peeps from the skirts of the wood,
I am mistress, no mother have I;
Yet blithe are my days, for my father is good,
And kind is my lover hard by;
They both work together beneath the green shade,
Both woodmen, my father and Joe.
Where I've listened whole hours to the echo that made
So much of a laugh or – *Halló*

From my basket at noon they expect their supply,
And with joy from my threshold I spring;
For the woodlands I love, and the oaks waring high,
And Echo that sings as I sing.
Though deep shades delight me, yet love is my food,
As I call the dear name of my Joe;
His musical shout is the pride of the wood,
And my heart leaps to hear the – *Halló*.

Simple flowers of the grove, little birds live at ease,
I wish not to wander from you;
I'll still dwell beneath the deep roar of your trees,
For I know that my Joe will be true.
The trill of the robin, the coo of the dove,
Are charms that I'll never forego;
But resting through life on the bosom of love,
Will remember the Woodland *Halló*.

– Robert Bloomfield

I Sat Among The Green Leaves

I sat among the green leaves, and heard the nuts falling,
    The blood-red butterflies were gold against the sun,
But in between the silence and the sweet birds calling
    The nuts fell one by one.

Why should they fall and the year but half over?
    Why should sorrow seek me and I so young and
        kind?
The leaf is on the bough and the dew is on the clover,
    But the green nuts are falling in the wind.

Oh, I gave my lips away and all my soul behind them.
    Why should trouble follow and the quick tears start?
The little birds may love and fly with only God to
    mind them,
    But the green nuts are falling on my heart.

– Marjorie L. C. Pickhall

The Flower

Once in a golden hour
    I cast to earth a seed.
Up there came a flower,
    The people said, a weed.

To and fro they went
    Thro' my garden-bower,
And muttering discontent
    Cursed me and my flower.

Then it grew so tall
    It wore a crown of light,
But thieves from o'er the wall
    Stole the seed by night.

Sowed it far and wide
    By every town and tower,
Till all the people cried,
    'Splendid is the flower.'

Read my little fable:
    He that runs may read.
Most can raise the flowers now,
    For all have got the seed.

And some are pretty enough,
    And some are poor indeed;
And now again the people
    Call it but a weed.

– Alfred, Lord Tennyson

A Little Nut-Tree

I had a little nut-tree, nothing would it bear
But a silver nutmeg and a golden pear;
The king of Spain's daughter came to visit me,
And all because of my little nut-tree.
I skipped over water, I danced over sea.
And all the birds in the air couldn't catch me.

– Anon

The Gardener

The gardener does not love to talk,
He makes me keep the gravel walk;
And when he puts his tools away,
He locks the door and takes the key.

Away behind the currant row
Where no one else but cook may go,
Far in the plots, I see him dig
Old and serious, brown and big.

He digs the flowers, green, red and blue,
Nor wishes to be spoken to.
He digs the flowers and cuts the hay,
And never seems to want to play.

Silly gardener! summer goes,
And winter comes with pinching toes,
When in the garden bare and brown
You must lay your barrow down.

Well now, and while the summer stays
To profit by these garden days
O how much wiser you would be
To play at Indian wars with me!

– *Robert Louis Stevenson*

Buttercups And Daisies

I never see a young hand hold
The starry bunch of white and gold,
But something warm and fresh will start
About the region of my heart; –
My smile expires into a sigh;
I feel a struggling in my eye,
'Twixt humid drop and sparkling ray,
Till rolling tears have won their way;
For, soul and brain will travel back,
Through memory's chequered mazes,
To days, when I but trod life's track
For buttercups and daisies.

There seems a bright and fairy spell
About their very names to dwell;
And though old Time has marked my brow
With care and thought, I love them now.
Smile, if you will, but some heartstrings
Are closest linked to simplest things;
And these wild flowers will hold mine fast,
Till love, and life, and all be past;

And then the only wish I have
Is, that the one who raises
The turf sod o'er me, plant my grave
With buttercups and daisies.

– *Eliza Cook*

All Things Bright And Beautiful

All things bright and beautiful,
All creatures great and small,
All things wise and wonderful:
The Lord God made them all.

Each little flower that opens,
Each little bird that sings,
God made their glowing colours,
And made their tiny wings.

The purple-headed mountains,
The river running by,
The sunset and the morning
That brightens up the sky.

The cold wind in the winter,
The pleasant summer sun,
The ripe fruits in the garden:
God made them every one.

God gave us eyes to see them,
And lips that we might tell
How great is God Almighty,
Who has made all things well.

– *Cecil Francis Alexander*

The Forest Reverie

'Tis said that when
The hands of men
Tamed this primeval wood,
And hoary trees with groans of woe,
Like warriors by an unknown foe,
Were in their strength subdued,
The virgin Earth gave instant birth
To springs that ne'er did flow
That in the sun did rivulets run,
And all around rare flowers did blow.
The wild rose pale perfumed the gale
And the queenly lily adown the dale
(Whom the sun and the dew
And the winds did woo),
With the gourd and the grape luxuriant grew.

So when in tears
The love of years
Is wasted like the snow,
And the fine fibrils of its life
By the rude wrong of instant strife

Are broken at a blow
Within the heart
Do springs upstart
Of which it doth now know,
And strange, sweet dreams,
Like silent streams
That from new fountains overflow,
With the earlier tide
Of rivers glide
Deep in the heart whose hope has died –
Quenching the fires its ashes hide –
Its ashes, whence will spring and grow
Sweet flowers, ere long,
The rare and radiant flowers of song!

– *Edgar Allan Poe*

The Cherry Trees

The cherry trees bend over and are shedding,
On the old road where all that passed are dead,
Their petals, strewing the grass as for a wedding
This early May morn when there is none to wed.

– *Edward Thomas*

By Wood And Wold

Lightly the breath of the spring wind blows,
    Though laden with faint perfume;
'Tis the fragrance rare that the bushman knows,
    The scent of the wattle bloom.
Two-thirds of our journey at least are done,
    Old horse! let us take a spell
In the shade from the glare of the noonday sun,
    Thus far we have travelled well;
Your bridle I'll slip, your saddle ungirth,
    And lay them beside this log,
For you'll roll in that track of reddish earth,
    And shake like a water-dog.

Upon yonder rise there's a clump of trees –
    Their shadows look cool and broad –
You can crop the grass as fast as you please,
    While I stretch my limbs on the sward;
'Tis pleasant, I ween, with a leafy screen
    O'er the weary head, to lie
On the mossy carpet of emerald green,
    'Neath the vault of the azure sky;

Thus all alone by the wood and wold,
　　I yield myself once again
To the memories old that, like tales fresh told,
　　Come flitting across the brain.

– *Adam Lindsay Gordon*

A Greenness O'er My Vision Passed

A greenness o'er my vision passed,
A freshness o'er my brain,
Rose up as when I saw them last
The glad green hills again.

Amid the streets' bewildering roar,
I heard the rushing stirs
Of vagrant breezes running o'er
The dark tops of the firs.

Far round, the wide and swooning view
The bound of chainèd heights;
Far off, the dales my footsteps knew,
With all their green delights;

Far down, the river winding through
The valley, silver white
Far up amid the cloudless blue
The slow sail of the kite.

A greenness o'er my vision passed,
A freshness o'er my brain,
Rose up as when I saw them last
The glad green hills again.

– *Isa Knox*

A Garden Song

Here in this sequestered close
Bloom the hyacinth and rose,
Here beside the modest stock
Flaunts the flaring hollyhock;
Here, without a pang, one sees
Ranks, conditions, and degrees.

All the seasons run their race
In this quiet resting-place;
Peach and apricot and fig
Here will ripen and grow big;
Here is store and overplus –
More had not Alcinoüs![1]

Here, in alleys cool and green,
Far ahead the thrush is seen;
Here along the southern wall
Keeps the bee his festival;
All is quiet else – afar
Sounds of toil and turmoil are.

---

1 Alcinoüs – a Phoenician King

Here be shadows large and long;
Here be spaces meet for song;
Grant, O garden-god, that I,
Now that none profane is nigh, –
Now that mood and moment please, –
Find the fair Pierides[1]!

– *Austin Dobson*

---

1 Pierides – a family of beautiful maidens

The Bush

Give us from dawn to dark,
Blue of Australian skies,
Let there be none to mark,
Whither our pathway lies.

Give us when noontime comes,
Rest in the woodland free –
Fragrant breath of the gums
Cold, sweet scent of the seas.

Give us the wattle's gold
And the dew-laden air,
And the loveliness bold
Loneliest landscape wear.

These are the haunts we love,
Glad with enchanted hours,
Bright as the heavens above,
Fresh as the wild bush flowers.

– James Lister Cuthbertson

Progress

They've builded wooden timber tracks,
And a trolley with screaming brakes
Noses into the secret bush,
Into the birdless brooding bush,
And the tall old gums it takes.
And down in the sunny valley,
The snorting saw screams slow;
O bush that nursed my people,
O bush that cursed my people,
That flayed and made my people,
I weep to watch you go.

– *Frank Wilmot*

Yea I Have A Goodly Heritage

My vineyard that is mine I have to keep,
Pruning for fruit the pleasant twigs and leaves.
Tend thou thy cornfield: one day thou shalt reap
In joy thy ripened sheaves.

Or if thine be an orchard, graft and prop
Food-bearing trees each watered in its place:
Or if a garden, let it yield for crop
Sweet herbs and herb of grace. –

But if my lot be sand where nothing grows? –
Nay, who hath said it? Tune a thankful psalm:
For though thy desert bloom not as the rose,
It yet can rear thy palm.

– *Christina Rossetti*

To Autumn

O Autumn, laden with fruit, and stained
With the blood of the grape, pass not, but sit
Beneath my shady roof; there thou may'st rest,
And tune thy jolly voice to my fresh pipe,
And all the daughters of the year shall dance!
Sing now the lusty song of fruits and flowers.

'The narrow bud opens her beauties to
The sun, and love runs in her thrilling veins;
Blossoms hang round the brows of Morning, and
Flourish down the bright cheek of modest Eve,
Till clustering Summer breaks forth into singing,
And feathered clouds strew flowers round her head.

'The spirits of the air live in the smells
Of fruit; and Joy, with pinions light, roves round
The gardens, or sits singing in the trees.'
Thus sang the jolly Autumn as he sat,
Then rose, girded himself, and o'er the bleak
Hills fled from our sight; but left his golden load.

– *William Blake*

I Haven't Told My Garden Yet

I haven't told my garden yet –
Lest that should conquer me.
I haven't quite the strength now
To break it to the Bee –

I will not name it in the street
For shops would stare at me –
That one so shy – so ignorant
Should have the face to die.

The hillsides must not know it –
Where I have rambled so –
Nor tell the loving forests
The day that I shall go –

Nor lisp it at the table –
Nor heedless by the way
Hint that within the Riddle
One will walk today.

– *Emily Dickinson*

A Fable

The mountain and the squirrel
Had a quarrel;
And the former called the latter 'Little Prig.'
Bun replied,
'You are doubtless very big;
But all sorts of things and weather
Must be taken in together
To make up a year
And a sphere.
And I think it's no disgrace
To occupy my place.
If I'm not so large as you,
You are not so small as I,
And not half so spry.
I'll not deny you make
A very pretty squirrel track;
Talents differ: all is well and wisely put;
If I cannot carry forests on my back,
Neither can you crack a nut.'

– *Ralph Waldo Emerson*

The Harvest Moon

It is the Harvest Moon! On gilded vanes
And roofs of villages, on woodland crests
And their aerial neighbourhoods of nests
Deserted, on the curtained window-panes
Of rooms where children sleep, on country lanes
And harvest-fields, its mystic splendour rests!
Gone are the birds that were our summer guests,
With the last sheaves return the labouring wains!
All things are symbols: the external shows
Of Nature have their image in the mind,
As flowers and fruits and falling of the leaves;
The song-birds leave us at the summer's close,
Only the empty nests are left behind,
And pipings of the quail among the sheaves.

– *Henry Wadsworth Longfellow*

Auf Wiedersehen – *Summer*

The little gate was reached at last,
Half hid in lilacs down the lane;
She pushed it wide, and, as she past,
A wistful look she backward cast,
And said, – '*Auf wiedersehen!*'

With hand on latch, a vision white
Lingered reluctant, and again
Half doubting if she did aright,
Soft as the dews that fell that night,
She said, – '*Auf wiedersehen!*'

The lamp's clear gleam flits up the stair;
I linger in delicious pain;
Ah, in that chamber, whose rich air
To breathe in thought I scarcely dare,
Thinks she, – '*Auf wiedersehen?*'

'Tis thirteen years; once more I press
The turf that silences the lane;
I hear the rustle of her dress,
I smell the lilacs, and – ah, yes,
I hear '*Auf wiedersehen!*'

Sweet piece of bashful maiden art!
The English words had seemed too fain,
But these – they drew us heart to heart,
Yet held us tenderly apart;
She said, '*Auf wiedersehen!*'

– James Russell Lowell

Paris

First, London, for its myriads; for its height,
Manhattan heaped in towering stalagmite;
But Paris for the smoothness of the paths
That lead the heart unto the heart's delight ...

Fair loiterer on the threshold of those days
When there's no lovelier prize the world displays
Than, having beauty and your twenty years,
You have the means to conquer and the ways,

And coming where the crossroads separate
And down each vista glories and wonders wait,
Crowning each path with pinnacles so fair
You know not which to choose, and hesitate –

Oh, go to Paris ... In the midday gloom
Of some old quarter take a little room
That looks off over Paris and its towers
From Saint Gervais round to the Emperor's Tomb –

So high that you can hear a mating dove
Croon down the chimney from the roof above,
See Notre Dame and know how sweet it is
To wake between Our Lady and our love.

And have a little balcony to bring
Fair plants to fill with verdure and blossoming,
That sparrows seek, to feed from pretty hands,
And swallows circle over in the Spring.

There of an evening you shall sit at ease
In the sweet month of flowering chestnut-trees,
There with your little darling in your arms,
Your pretty dark-eyed Manon or Louise.

And looking out over the domes and towers
That chime the fleeting quarters and the hours,
While the bright clouds banked eastward back of them
Blush in the sunset, pink as hawthorn flowers,

You cannot fail to think, as I have done,
Some of life's ends attained, so you be one
Who measures life's attainment by the hours
That Joy has rescued from oblivion.

– Alan Seeger

Hope

We speak with the lip, and we dream in the soul,
Of some better and fairer day;
And our days, the meanwhile, to that golden goal
Are gliding and sliding away.
Now the world becomes old, now again it is young,
But "The better"'s forever the word on the tongue.

At the threshold of life hope leads us in –
Hope plays round the mirthful boy;
Though the best of its charms may with youth begin,
Yet for age it reserves its toy.

– Friedrich Schiller
(translator untraced)

Epitaph

Here lies a poor woman who was always tired;
She lived in a house where help was not hired.
Her last words on earth were: 'Dear friends, I am going
Where washing ain't done, nor sweeping, no sewing:
But everything there is exact to my wishes;
For where they don't eat there's no washing of dishes ...
Don't mourn for me now; don't mourn for me never –
I'm going to do nothing for ever and ever.'

– *Anon*

Life

We are born; we laugh; we weep;
We love; we droop; we die!
Ah! wherefore do we laugh or weep?
Why do we live, or die?
Who knows that secret deep?
    Alas, not I!

Why doth the violet spring
Unseen by human eye?
Why do the radiant seasons bring
Sweet thoughts that quickly fly?
Why do our fond hearts cling
    To things that die?

We toil, – through pain and wrong;
We fight, – and fly;
We love; we lose; and then, ere long,
Stone-dead we lie.
O life! is all thy song
    'Endure and – die'?

– *Barry Cornwall*

Tears, Idle Tears

    Tears, idle tears, I know not what they mean,
Tears from the depth of some divine despair
Rise in the heart, and gather to the eyes,
In looking on the happy autumn-fields,
And thinking of the days that are no more.

    Fresh as the first beam glittering on a sail,
That brings our friends up from the underworld,
Sad as the last which reddens over one
That sinks with all we love below the verge;
So sad, so fresh, the days that are no more.

    Ah, sad and strange as in dark summer dawns
The earliest pipe of half-awakened birds
To dying ears, when unto dying eyes
The casement slowly grows a glimmering square;
So sad, so strange, the days that are no more.

Dear as remembered kisses after death,
And sweet as those by hopeless fancy feign'd
On lips that are for others; deep as love,
Deep as first love, and wild with all regret;
O Death in Life, the days that are no more!

– *Alfred, Lord Tennyson*

On His Blindness

When I consider how my light is spent
Ere half my days in this dark world and wide,
And that one talent which is death to hide
Lodged with me useless, though my soul more bent
To serve therewith my Maker, and present
My true account, lest he returning chide,
'Doth God exact day-labour, light denied?'
I fondly ask. But Patience, to prevent
That murmur, soon replies: 'God doth not need
Either man's work or his own gifts: who best
Bear his mild yoke, they serve him best. His state
Is kingly; thousands at his bidding speed
And post o'er land and ocean without rest:
They also serve who only stand and wait.'

– *John Milton*

My Aunt

My aunt! my dear unmarried aunt!
Long years have o'er her flown;
Yet still she strains the aching clasp
That binds her virgin zone;
I know it hurts her, – though she looks
As cheerful as she can;
Her waist is ampler than her life,
For life is but a span.

My aunt! my poor deluded aunt!
Her hair is almost grey;
Why will she train that winter curl
In such a spring-like way?
How can she lay her glasses down,
And say she reads as well,
When through a double convex lens
She just makes out to spell?

Her father – grandpapa! forgive
This erring lip its smiles –
Vowed she should make the finest girl
Within a hundred miles;
He sent her to a stylish school
'T was in her thirteenth June;
And with her, as the rules required,
'Two towels and a spoon.'

They braced my aunt against a board,
To make her straight and tall;
They laced her up, they starved her down,
To make her light and small;
They pinched her feet, they singed her hair,
They screwed it up with pins; –
Oh, never mortal suffered more
In penance for her sins.

So, when my precious aunt was done,
My grandsire brought her back
(By daylight, lest some rabid youth
Might follow on the track);
'Ah!' said my grandsire, as he shook
Some powder in his pan,
'What could this lovely creature do
Against a desperate man!'

Alas! nor chariot, nor barouche,
Nor bandit cavalcade,
Tore from the trembling father's arms
His all-accomplished maid.
For her how happy had it been!
And Heaven had spared to me
To see one sad, ungathered rose
On my ancestral tree.

– *Oliver Wendell Holmes*

A Letter From The Front

I was out early to-day, spying about
From the top of a haystack – such a lovely morning –
And when I mounted again to canter back
I saw across a field in the broad sunlight
A young Gunner Subaltern, stalking along
With a rook-rifle held at the ready, and – would you
    believe it? –
A domestic cat, soberly marching beside him.

So I laughed, and felt quite well disposed to the
    youngster,
And shouted out 'the top of the morning' to him,
And wished him 'Good sport!' – and then I
    remembered
My rank, and his, and what I ought to be doing:
And I rode nearer, and added, 'I can only suppose
You have not seen the Commander-in-Chief's order
Forbidding English officers to annoy their Allies
By hunting and shooting.'
But he stood and saluted
And said earnestly, 'I beg your pardon, Sir,

I was only going out to shoot a sparrow
To feed my cat with.'
So there was the whole picture,
The lovely early morning, the occasional shell
Screeching and scattering past us, the empty
    landscape, –
Empty, except for the young Gunner saluting,
And the cat, anxiously watching his every movement.

I may be wrong, or I may have told it badly,
But it struck me as being extremely ludicrous.

— *Sir Henry Newbolt*

On The Ball[1]

In the days to call, which we have left behind,
Our boyhood's glorious game,
And our youthful vigour has declined
With its mirth and its lonesome end;
You will think of the time, the happy time,
Its memories fond recall
When in the bloom of your youthful prime
We've kept upon the ball

Kick off, throw in, have a little scrimmage,
Keep it low, a splendid rush, bravo, win or die;
On the ball, City, never mind the danger,
Steady on, now's your chance,
Hurrah! We've scored a goal.

Let all tonight then drink with me
To the football game we love,
And wish it may successful be

---

1 ' On The Ball' – Norwich City FC song – the oldest football song in British history

And in one grand united toast
Join player, game and song
And fondly pledge your pride and toast
Success to the City club.

Kick off, throw in, have a little scrimmage,
Keep it low, a splendid rush, bravo, win or die;
On the ball, City, never mind the danger,
Steady on, now's your chance,
Hurrah! We've scored a goal.

– *Anon*

Good And Clever

If all the good people were clever,
    And all clever people were good,
The world would be nicer than ever
    We thought that it possibly could.

But somehow 'tis seldom or never
    The two hit it off as they should,
The good are so harsh to the clever,
    The clever, so rude to the good!

So friends, let it be our endeavour
    To make each by each understood;
For few can be good, like the clever,
    Or clever, so well as the good.

– *Elizabeth Wordsworth*

A Criticism Of Critics

How often have the critics, trained
To look upon the sky
Through telescopes securely chained,
Forgot the naked eye.

Within the compass of their glass
Each smallest star they knew,
And not a meteor could pass
But they were looking through.

When a new planet shed its rays
Beyond their field of vision,
And simple folk ran out to gaze,
They laughed in high derision.

They railed upon the senseless throng
Who cheered the brave new light.
And yet the learned men were wrong,
The simple folk were right.

– *Robert Fuller Murray*

A Poet's Thought

Tell me, what is a poet's thought?
Is it on the sudden born?
Is it from the starlight caught?
Is it by the tempest taught,
Or by whispering morn?

Was it cradled in the brain?
Chained awhile, or nursed in night?
Was it wrought with toil and pain?
Did it bloom and fade again,
Ere it burst to light?

No more question of its birth:
Rather love its better part!
'Tis a thing of sky and earth,
Gathering all its golden worth
From the Poet's heart.

– *Barry Cornwall*

The Flower Of Mending

When Dragon-fly would fix his wings,
When Snail would patch his house,
When moths have marred the overcoat
Of tender Mister Mouse,

The pretty creatures go with haste
To the sunlit blue-grass hills
Where the Flower of Mending yields the wax
And webs to help their ills.

The hour the coats are waxed and webbed
They fall into a dream,
And when they wake the ragged robes
Are joined without a seam.

My heart is but a dragon-fly,
My heart is but a mouse,
My heart is but a haughty snail
In a little stony house.

Your hand Your voice a web to bind.
You were a Mending Flower to me
To cure my heart and mind.

– *Vachel Lindsay*

The Sewing Bee

On a wintry afternoon
They bring their work
And settle round the hearth
A faint half circle of ladylike emotions
Withered now and near the end
They sit embroidering with fine silk of remembrance
Samples of my past history.
Their crackling gossip pricks like splintered glass.
When I go in they flutter to me yearning and coquettish
I am amused to speak in a bold voice
Indelicate truths, rich in blood red oaths
And when they are shocked away
To sprawl alone full lengthened and masculine
Filling my pipe with dark strong thoughts
On the emancipation of woman flesh or sprite.

– *Jeanne d'Orge*

See The Kitten On The Wall

See the kitten on the wall,
Sporting with the leaves that fall.
Withered leaves – one – two – three
From the lofty elder tree.
Though the calm and frosty air,
Of this morning bright and fair.
Eddying round and round they sink,
Softly, slowly; one might think.
From the motions that are made,
Every little leaf conveyed
Sylph or Faery hither tending,
To this lower world descending.
Each invisible and mute,
In his wavering parachute.

But the kitten, how she starts,
Crouches, stretches, paws, and darts!
First at one, and then its fellow,
Just as light and just as yellow.
There are many now – now one,
Now they stop and there are none.

What intenseness of desire,
In her upward eye of fire!
With a tiger-leap half-way,
Now she meets the coming prey.
Lets it go as fast, and then;
Has it in her power again.

Now she works with three or four,
Like an Indian conjurer;
Quick as he in feats of art,
Far beyond in joy of heart.
Where her antics played in the eye,
Of a thousand standers-by,
Clapping hands with shout and stare,
What would little Tabby care
For the plaudits of the crowd?

– William Wordsworth

The Poet's Calendar: September

I bear the Scales, where hang in equipoise
The night and day; and when unto my lips
I put my trumpet, with its stress and noise
Fly the white clouds like tattered sails of ships;
The tree-tops lash the air with sounding whips;
Southward the clamorous sea-fowl wing their flight;
The hedges are all red with haws and hips,
The Hunter's Moon reigns empress of the night.

— *Henry Wadsworth Longfellow*

The Cat And The Moon

The cat went here and there
and the moon spun round like a top,
and the nearest kin of the moon,
the creeping cat, looked up.
Black Minnaloushe stared at the moon,
for, wander and wail as he would,
the pure cold light in the sky
troubled his animal blood.

Minnaloushe runs in the grass
lifting his delicate feet.
Do you dance, Minnaloushe, do you dance?
When two close kindred meet,
what better than call a dance?
Maybe the moon may learn,
tired of that courtly fashion,
a new dance turn.

Minnaloushe creeps through the grass
from moonlit place to place,
the sacred moon overhead

has taken a new phase.
Does Minnaloushe know that his pupils
will pass from change to change,
and that from round to crescent,
from crescent to round they range?

Minnaloushe creeps through the grass
alone, important and wise,
and lifts to the changing moon
his changing eyes.

– *W. B. Yeats*

Be Your Words Made

Be your words made, good Sir, of Indian ware,
That you allow me them by so small rate?
Or do you cutted[1] Spartans imitate?
Or do you mean my tender ears to spare
That to my questions you so total are?
When I demand of Phoenix Stella's state,
You say, forsooth, you left her well of late:
O God, think you that satisfies my care?
I would know whether she did sit or walk;
How clothed; how waited on; sighed she or smiled;
Whereof, with whom, how often did she talk;
With what pastime time's journey she beguiled;
If her lips deigned to sweeten my poor name:
Say all; and all well said, still say the same.

– Sir Philip Sydney

---

1 cutted – curt or rude

A Time To Talk

When a friend calls to me from the road
And slows his horse to a meaning walk,
I don't stand still and look around
On all the hills I haven't hoed,
And shout from where I am, What is it?
No, not as there is a time to talk.
I thrust my hoe in the mellow ground,
Blade-end up and five feet tall,
And plod: I go up to the stone wall
For a friendly visit.

— *Robert Frost*

A Gargoyle On Notre Dame

With angel's wings and brutish-human form,
Weathered with centuries of sun and storm,
He crouches yonder on the gallery wall,
Monstrous, superb, indifferent, cynical:
And all the pulse of Paris cannot stir
Her one immutable philosopher.

— *Edmund Kemper Broadus*

I Sing Of A Maiden

I sing of a maiden
That is matchless,
King of all kings
For her son she chose.

He came as still
Where his mother was
As dew in April
That falls on the grass.

He came as still
To his mother's bower
As dew in April
That falls on the flower.

He came as still
Where his mother lay
As dew in April
That falls on the spray.

Mother and maiden
There was never, ever one but she;
Well may such a lady
God's mother be.

– *Anon*

An Astrologer's Song

To the Heavens above us
Oh, look and behold
The planets that love us
All harnessed in gold!
What chariots, what horses,
Against us shall bide
While the Stars in their courses
Do fight on our side?

All thought, all desires,
That are under the sun,
Are one with their fires,
As we also are one;
All matter, all spirit,
All fashion, all frame,
Receive and inherit
Their strength from the same.

Earth quakes in her throes
And we wonder for why!
But the blind planet knows

When her ruler is nigh;
And, attuned since Creation,
To perfect accord,
She thrills in her station
And yearns to her Lord.

Then, doubt not, ye fearful –
The Eternal is King –
Up, heart, and be cheerful,
And lustily sing:
What chariots, what horses,
Against us shall bide
While the Stars in their courses
Do fight on our side?

– Rudyard Kipling

Not From The Stars...

Not from the stars do I my judgment pluck;
And yet methinks I have astronomy,
But not to tell of good or evil luck,
Of plagues, of dearths[1], or seasons' quality;
Nor can I fortune to brief minutes tell,
Pointing to each his thunder, rain and wind,
Or say with princes if it shall go well,
By oft predict that I in heaven find:
But from thine eyes my knowledge I derive,
And, constant stars, in them I read such art
As truth and beauty shall together thrive,
If from thyself to store thou wouldst convert;
Or else of thee this I prognosticate:
Thy end is truth's and beauty's doom and date.

– *William Shakespeare*

---

1 dearth – scarcity, shortage

Index

Alcott, Louisa May	A Song From The Suds	47
Alexander, Cecil Francis	All Things Bright And Beautiful	72
Anon	A Little Nut-Tree	67
	Epitaph	95
	On The Ball	105
	I Sing Of A Maiden	121
Baillie, Joanna	The Maid Of Llanwellyn	54
Bayly, Thomas Haynes	Why Don't The Men Propose	49
Blake, William	To Autumn	86
Bloomfield, Robert	The Woodland *Halló*	62
Breton, Nicholas	Phillida And Corydon	33
Broadus, Edmund Kemper	A Gargoyle On Notre Dame	120
Brooke, Rupert	Sonnet	8
	The Young Man In April	28
Bryant, William Cullen	O Fairest Of The Rural Maids	52
Carew, Thomas	Good Counsel To A Young Maid	2
Cook, Eliza	Buttercups And Daisies	70
Cornwall, Barry	Life	96
	A Poet's Thought	109
Cuthbertson, James Lister	The Bush	83
de Vere, Aubrey	Love's Spite	18
Dickinson, Emily	I Haven't Told My Garden Yet	87
Dobson, Austin	A Garden Song	81

Donne, John	Love's Infiniteness	4
d'Orge, Jeanne	The Sewing Bee	112
Emerson, Ralph Waldo	A Fable	88
Fletcher, John	Hear, Ye Ladies	36
Frost, Robert	Gathering Leaves	58
	A Time To Talk	119
Gay, John	If Love The Virgin's Heart Invade	25
Gilmore, Mary	Marri'd	44
Goldsmith, Oliver	Women	6
Gordon, Adam Lindsay	By Wood And Wold	77
Hardy, Thomas	She Charged Me	30
Hart, Lorenz	If They Asked Me, I Could Write A Book	24
Herrick, Robert	No Loathsomeness In Love	22
Holmes, Oliver Wendell	My Aunt	100
Jonson, Ben	Song	12
Keats, John	Song	14
	Nymph	23
	I Stood Tip-Toe	56
Kipling, Rudyard	An Astrologer's Song	123
Knox, Isa	A Greenness O'er My Vision Passed	79
Lee, Muna	When We Shall Be Dust	7
Lindsay, Vachel	The Flower Of Mending	110
Longfellow, Henry Wadsworth	The Harvest Moon	89
	The Poet's Calendar: September	115
Lowell, James Russell	*Auf Wiedersehen* – Summer	90
Marston, Philip Bourke	Her Pity	16
Milton, John	On His Blindness	99
Moore, Thomas	Did Not	20
Murray, Robert Fuller	A Criticism Of Critics	108
Neilson, John Shaw	Love's Coming	38
Newbolt, Sir Henry	A Letter From The Front	103
Norton, Grace Fallow	Love Is A Terrible Thing	9

Pickhall, Marjorie L. C.	I Sat Among The Green Leaves	64
Poe, Edgar Allan	The Forest Reverie	74
Pope, Alexander	On A Certain Lady At Court	1
Prior, Matthew	A Song	21
Procter, Adelaide Anne	A Woman's Question	40
Rossetti, Christina	Yea I Have A Goodly Heritage	85
Schiller, Friedrich	Hope	94
Seeger, Alan	Paris	92
Shakespeare, William	Being Your Slave, What Should I Do?	32
	Not From The Stars . . .	125
Shelley, Percy Bysshe	I Fear Thy Kisses	13
	Love's Philosophy	43
Stevenson, Robert Louis	The Gardener	68
Story, William Wetmore	Snowdrop	11
Sydney, Sir Philip	Be Your Words Made	118
Synge, J. M.	On An Island	46
Lord Tennyson, Alfred	O That 'Twere Possible	29
	The Flower	65
	Tears, Idle Tears	97
Thomas, Edward	The Cherry Trees	76
Wilmot, Frank	Progress	84
Wordsworth, Elizabeth	Good And Clever	107
Wordsworth, William	Louisa	26
	To A Young Lady Who Had Been Reproached For Taking Long Walks In The Country	60
	See The Kitten On The Wall	113
Yeats, W. B.	The Cat And The Moon	116

Derek & Julia Parker

Derek and Julia Parker became internationally famous with the publication of *The Compleat Astrologer* in 1971, the first thorough modern text-book of astrology. A world-wide best-seller, with a new edition released in 1984, it remained in print for twenty years until replaced by *Parkers' Astrology*. Julia Parker remains an active astrologer; Derek (who for five years edited the UK's *Poetry Review*) is also a biographer. They have jointly written books on dream interpretation, popular psychology, travel, the theatre, magic – and love. In 2002, after forty years of working in London, they emigrated to Sydney, where they live with their two wire-haired terriers, Fille and Crim.

Loved the book?

Join thousands of other readers online at

AUSTRALIAN READERS:

randomhouse.com.au/talk

NEW ZEALAND READERS:

randomhouse.co.nz/talk